2 KINDS OF PEOPLE

A VISUAL COMPATIBILITY QUIZ

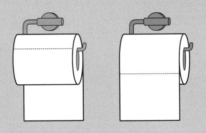

JOÃO ROCHA

Workman Publishing · New York

Library of Congress Cataloging-in-Publication Data is available.
ISBN: 978-0-7611-8949-7

Book design by Ariana Abud

Workman books are available at special discounts when purchased in bulk for premiums
and sales promotions as well as for fund-raising or educational use. Special editions or
book excerpts can also be created to specification. For details, contact the Special Sales
Director at the address below, or send an email to specialmarkets@workman.com.

Workman Publishing Co., Inc.
225 Varick Street
New York, NY 10014-4381
workman.com

WORKMAN is a registered trademark of Workman Publishing Co., Inc.

Printed in China

First printing July 2017

10 9 8 7 6 5 4 3 2

To Rita,
my opposite and yet my equal.

INTRODUCTION

There are only two kinds of people in this world, or so the saying goes. 2 Kinds of People also happens to be the name of an illustration project that started out as a Tumblr and has now found its way into the physical world in the form of the innocent-looking book that you are holding right now. But this book is no ordinary piece of literature: Inside, you will find yourself and everybody you have ever known. You might approach the book as a game, but it is very much a tool—a way to find out how you connect to the people around you, and discover how similar you are to your friends, family, or that coworker who hoards all the sticky notes and refuses to share them with anyone.

The project began, oddly enough, with laundry: in my wife's point of view, I have a total inability to do it properly. While I admit that my technique is far from perfect, it simply feels the most practical to me. The more I observed these tiny differences that set us apart, the more intrigued I became. And so I began illustrating them as a way to chronicle and explore personal subtleties that are interesting precisely *because* they're so prevalent in our daily lives. What started off as a just-for-fun side project ultimately taught me all kinds of things about myself, love, world peace, and what is argued by some to be the correct way—and indeed the only way—to eat pizza. It also taught me something wonderful about people: that you can be totally unrelated to someone, and yet you will almost certainly find that the two of you have at least one thing in common.

In the end, there are no right or wrong answers. These illustrations merely depict universal commonalities among people of all races, religions, genders, sexual orientations, nationalities, and ages. This book is not about our visual or structural differences; rather, a celebration of human interaction and connectivity.

So, now that we've got the introduction out of the way, let's get to know you . . .

HOW TO PLAY

1. Pick a partner.

2. Turn the page to the first spread. Each person chooses which illustration best fits his or her personality.

3. If it's a match, record it on the foldout scoring wheel in the back by moving the spinner forward one space. If it's not a match, continue to the next spread.

4. When you reach the end of the book, check the scoring wheel for your final match number.

5. Find that number on the Scale of Compatibility to discover if you're mortal enemies, casual cohorts, soul mates, or somewhere in between.

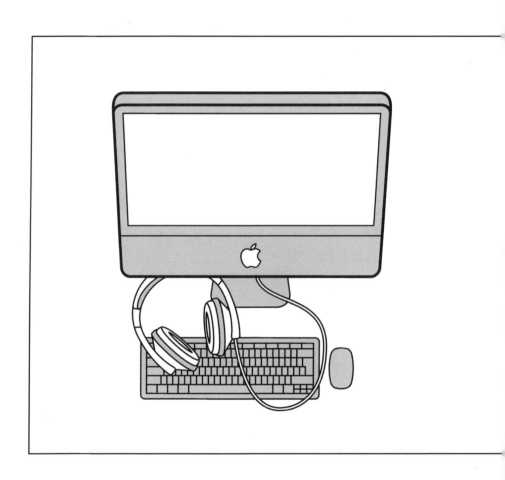

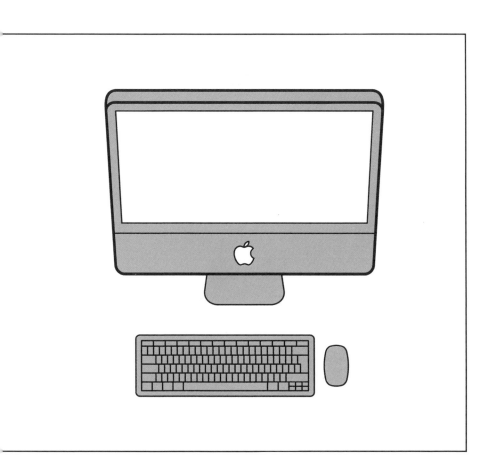

07:00
Alarm

07:20
Alarm

07:35
Alarm

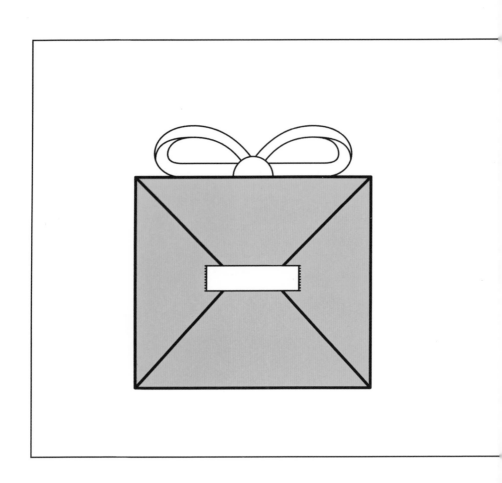

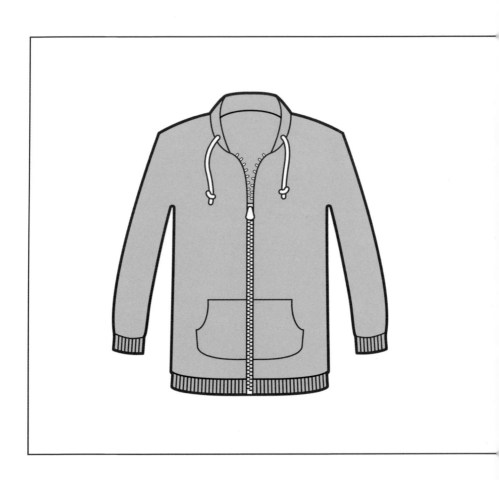

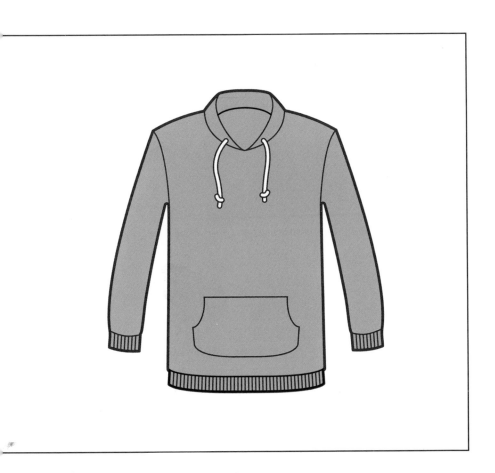

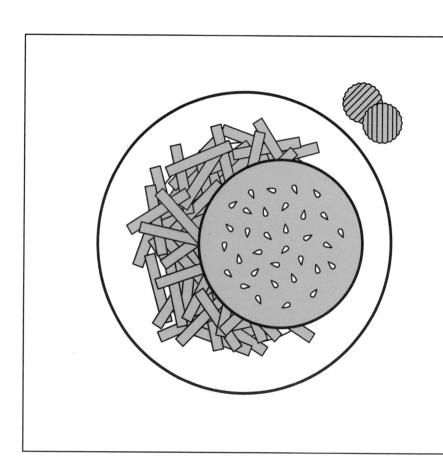

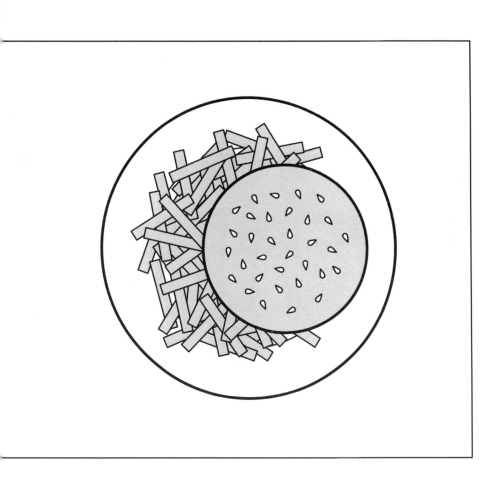

From:

_____
_____
_____

Place
stamp
here

NYC Department of Finance
Parking Violations
1407 Graymalkin Lane
Salem Center, New York

Bill Murray SIGNATURE

SIGNATURE

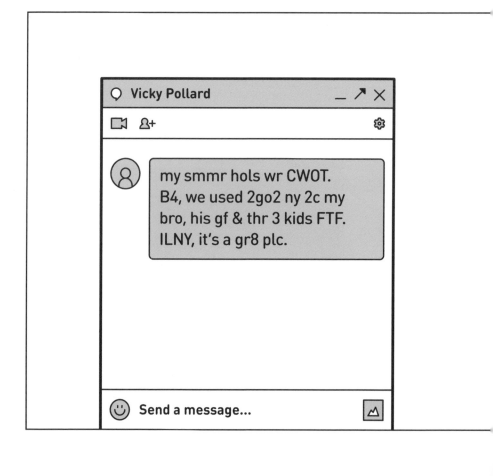

Vicky Pollard

My summer holidays were a complete waste of time. Before, we used to go to New York to see my brother, his girlfriend, and their three kids face to face. I love New York. It's a great place.

Send a message...

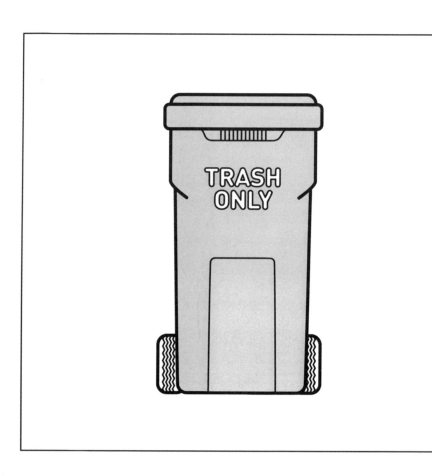

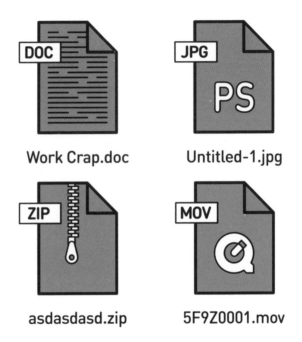

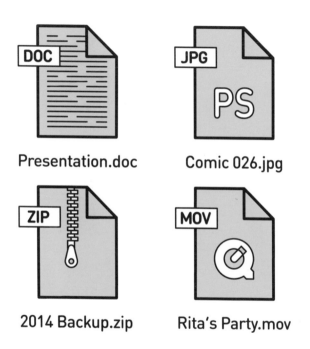

Presentation.doc

Comic 026.jpg

2014 Backup.zip

Rita's Party.mov

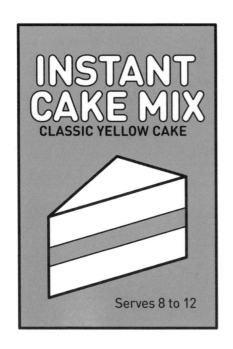

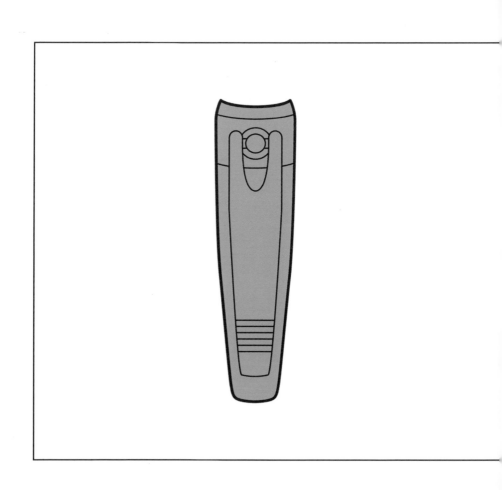

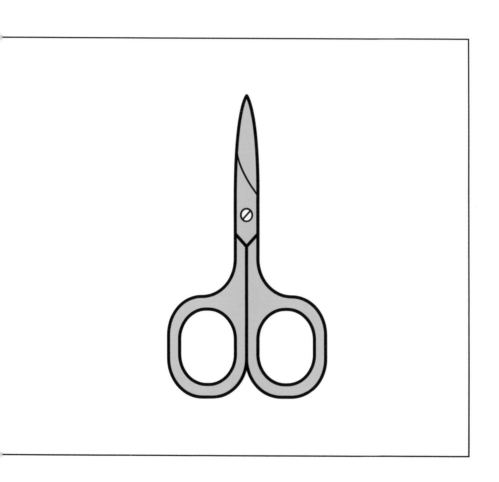

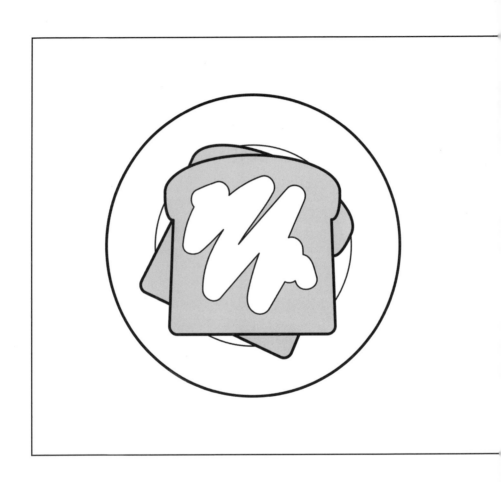

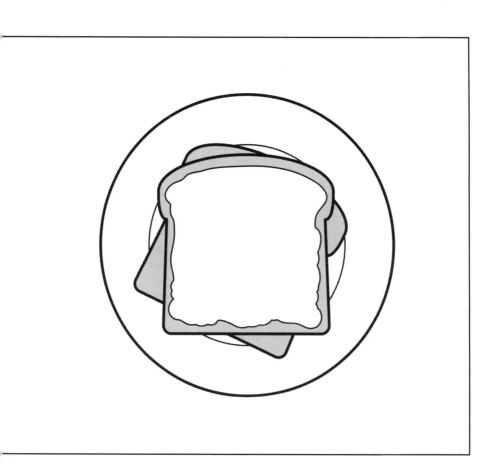

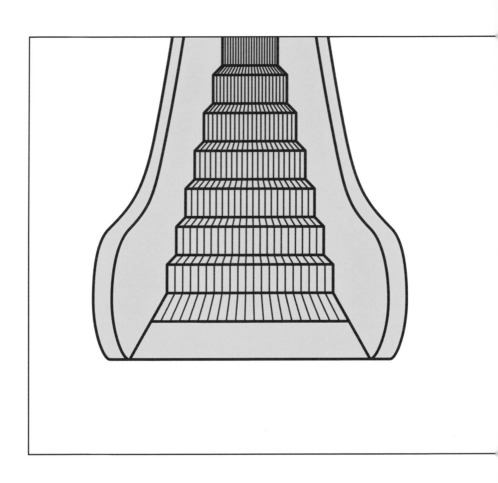

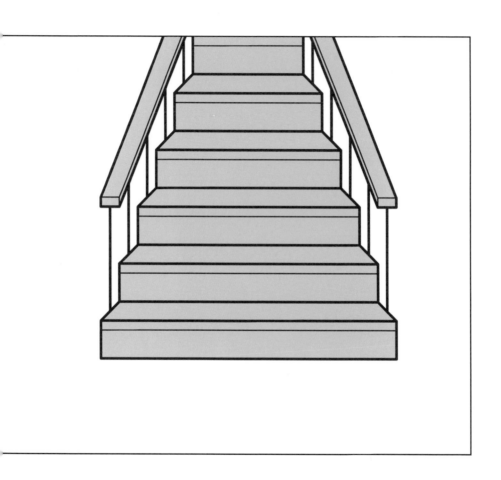

CINEMA P...
STAR WARS: THE

RATING: PG-13
$5 RECEIPT

THU   12/18/2015
SHOWING   12:35PM
AUD. 8   SEAT 22A

HERSHEY'S
MILK CHOCOLATE

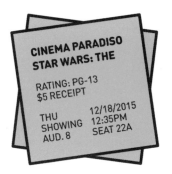

CINEMA PARADISO
STAR WARS: THE

RATING: PG-13
$5 RECEIPT

THU   12/18/2015
SHOWING   12:35PM
AUD. 8   SEAT 22A

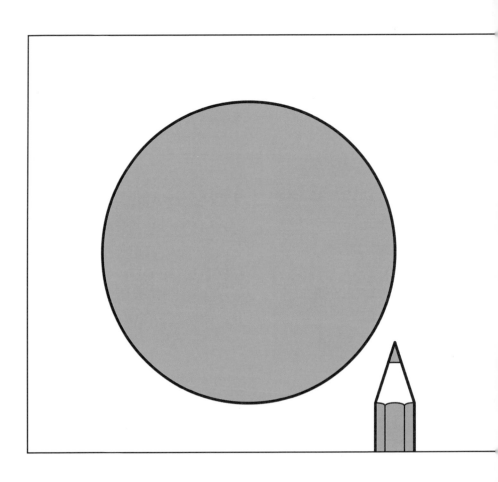

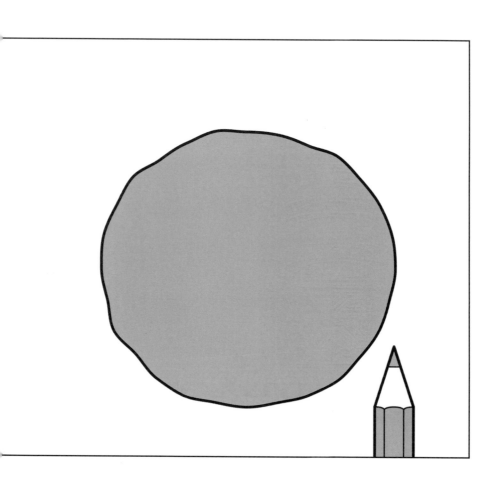

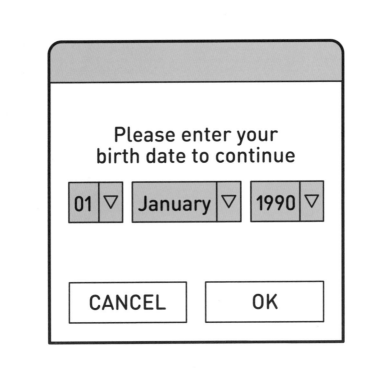

Please enter your
birth date to continue

01 ▽   January ▽   1990 ▽

CANCEL   OK

Please enter your
birth date to continue

18 ▽   May   ▽   1985 ▽

CANCEL   OK

HEINZ

TOMATO
KETCHUP

NET WT
14OZ (397g)

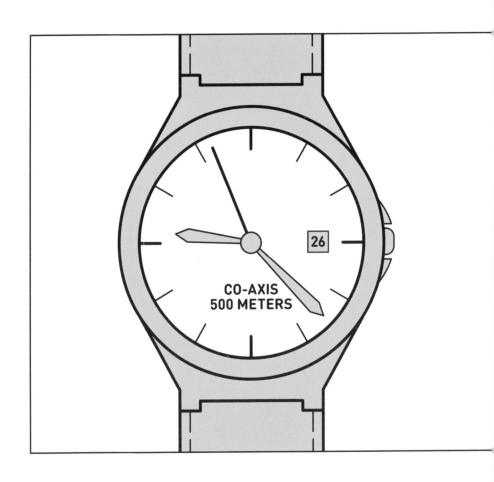

CO-AXIS
500 METERS

26

09:22
Tuesday, January 26

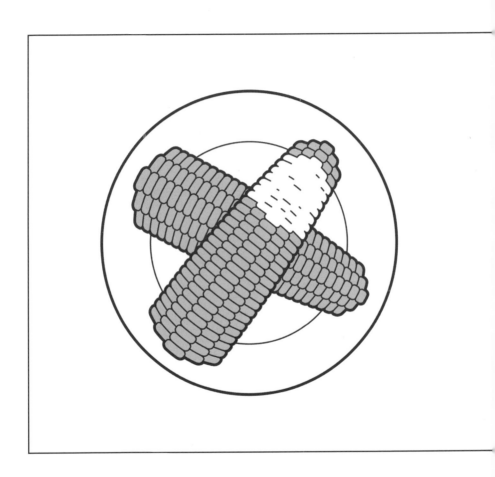

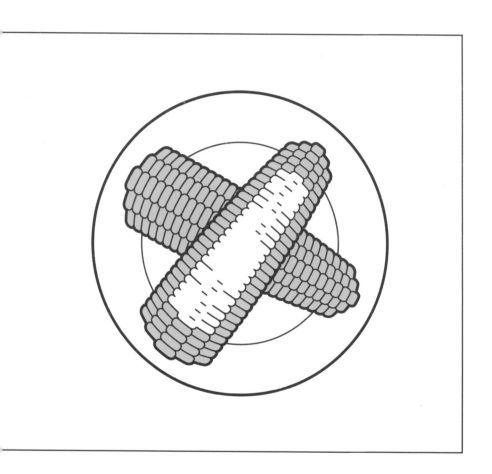

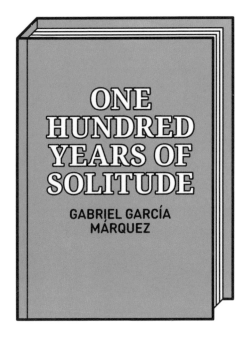

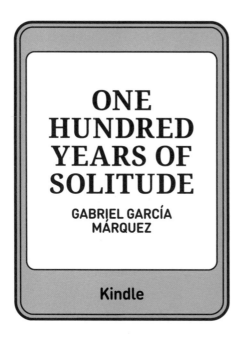

ONE
HUNDRED
YEARS OF
SOLITUDE

GABRIEL GARCÍA
MÁRQUEZ

Kindle

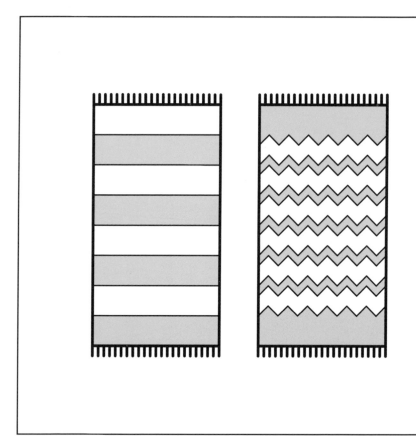

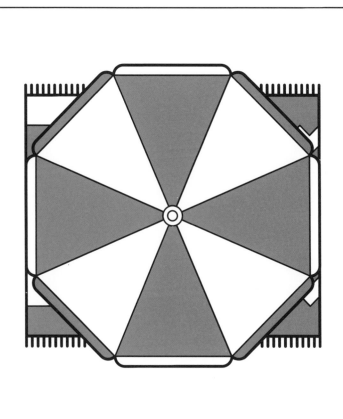

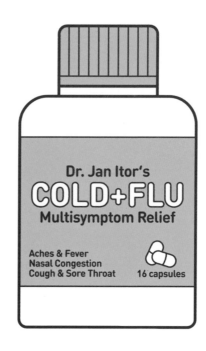

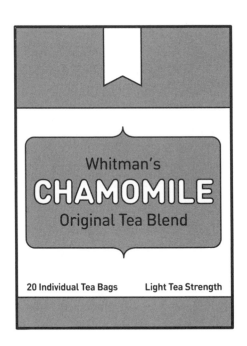

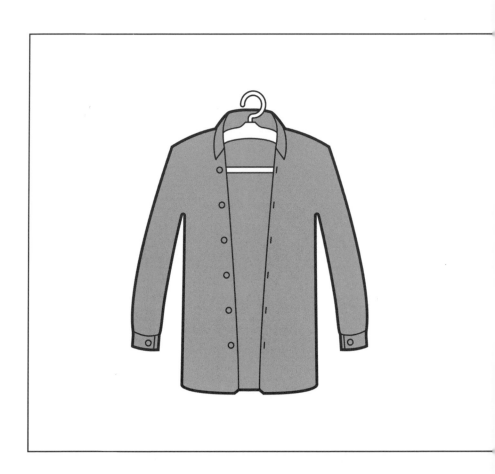

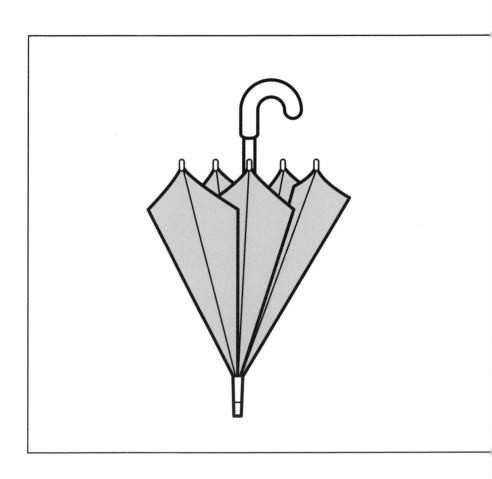

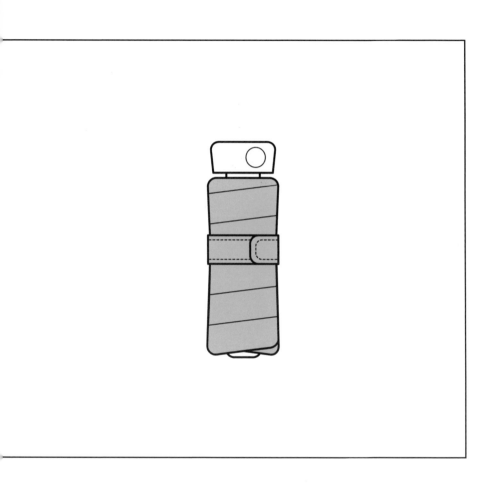

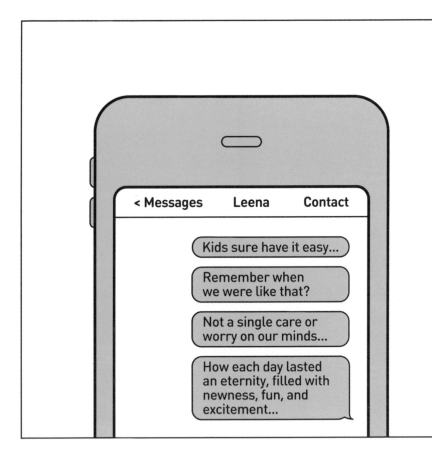

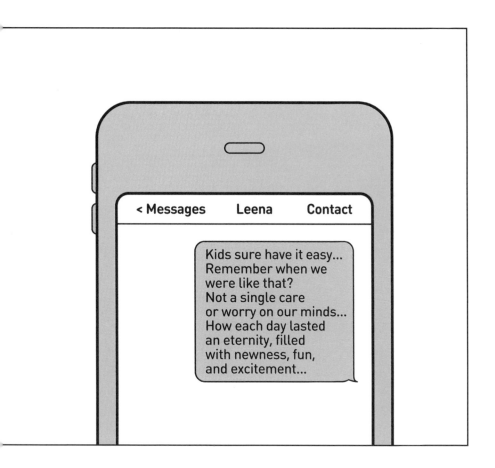

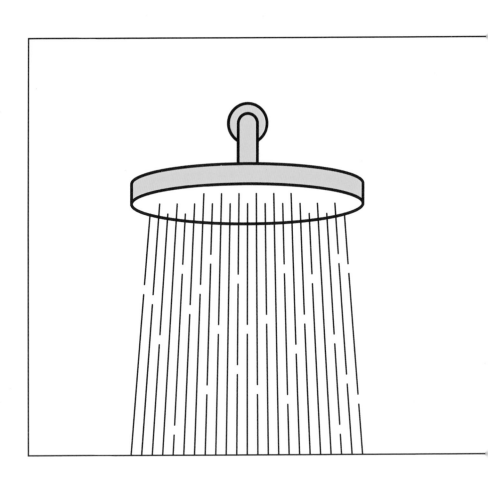

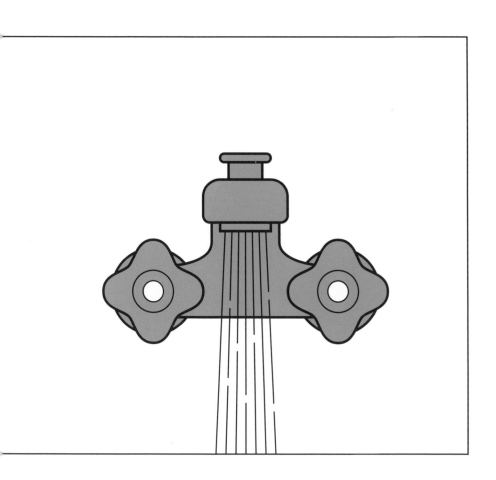

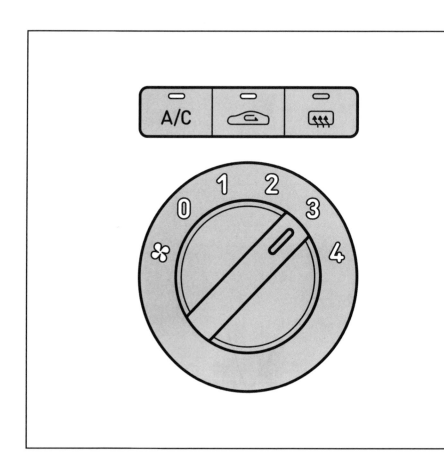

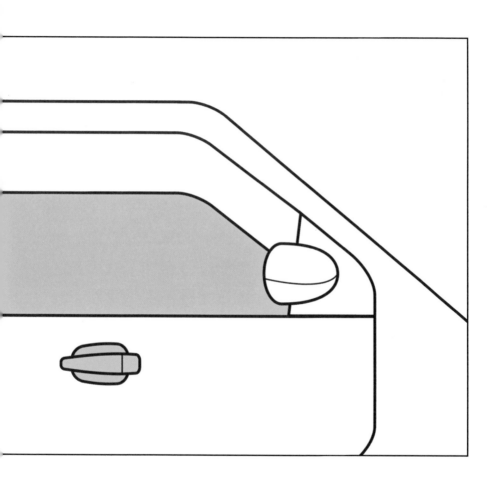

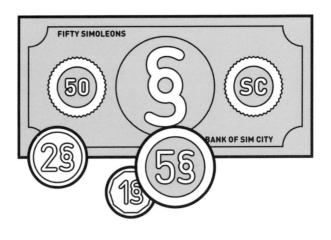

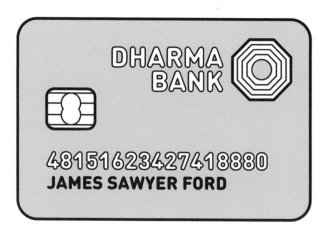

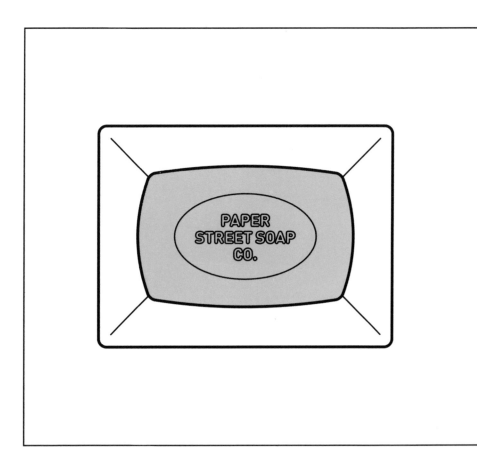

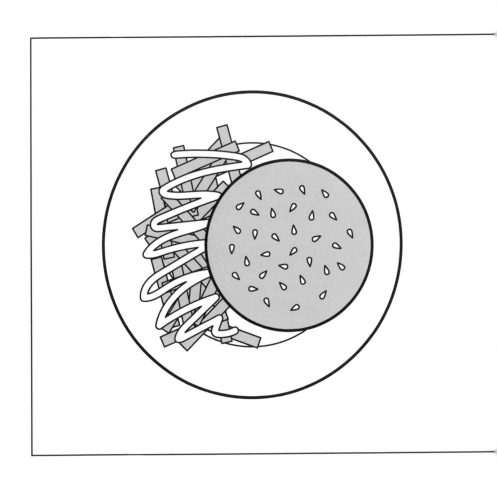

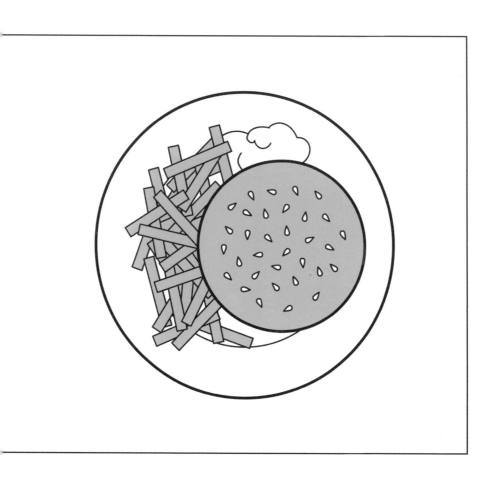

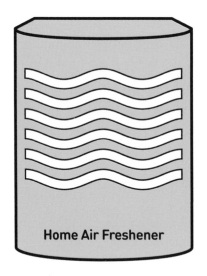

Home Air Freshener

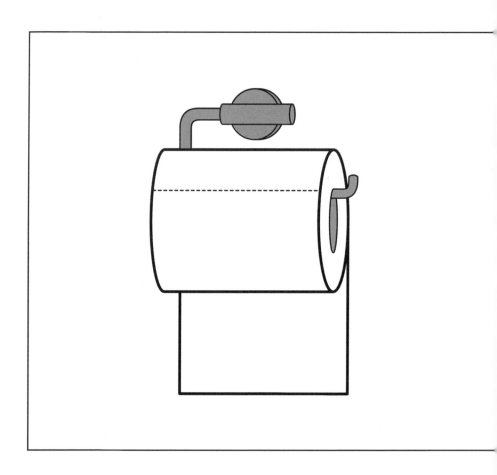

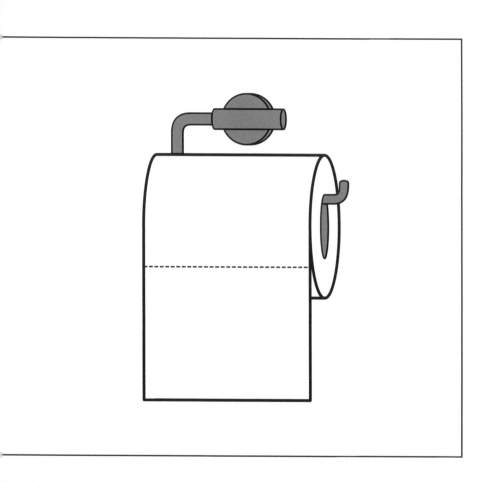

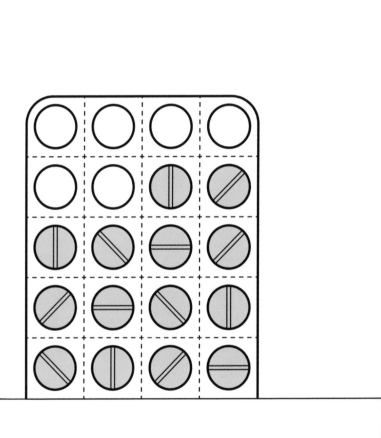

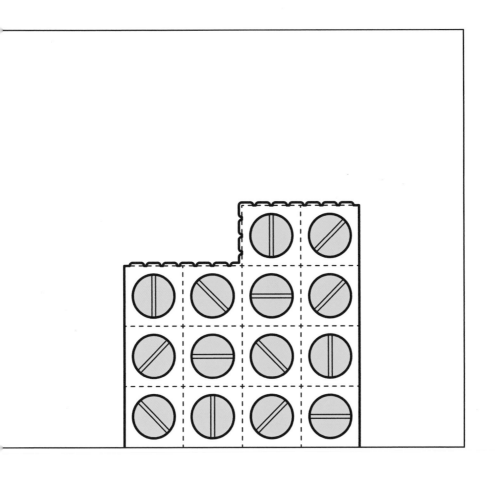

Clash

Temple

Vine

WhatsApp

Clear

Podcast

Bē

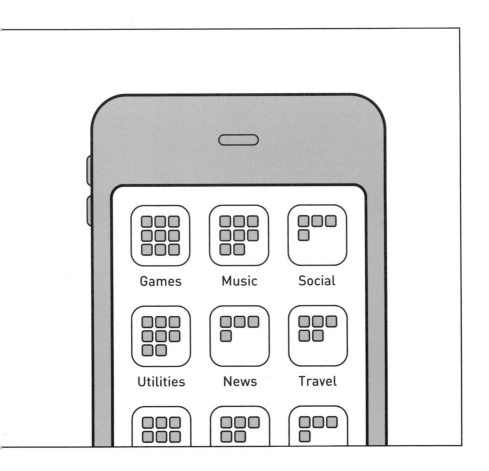

Games

Music

Social

Utilities

News

Travel

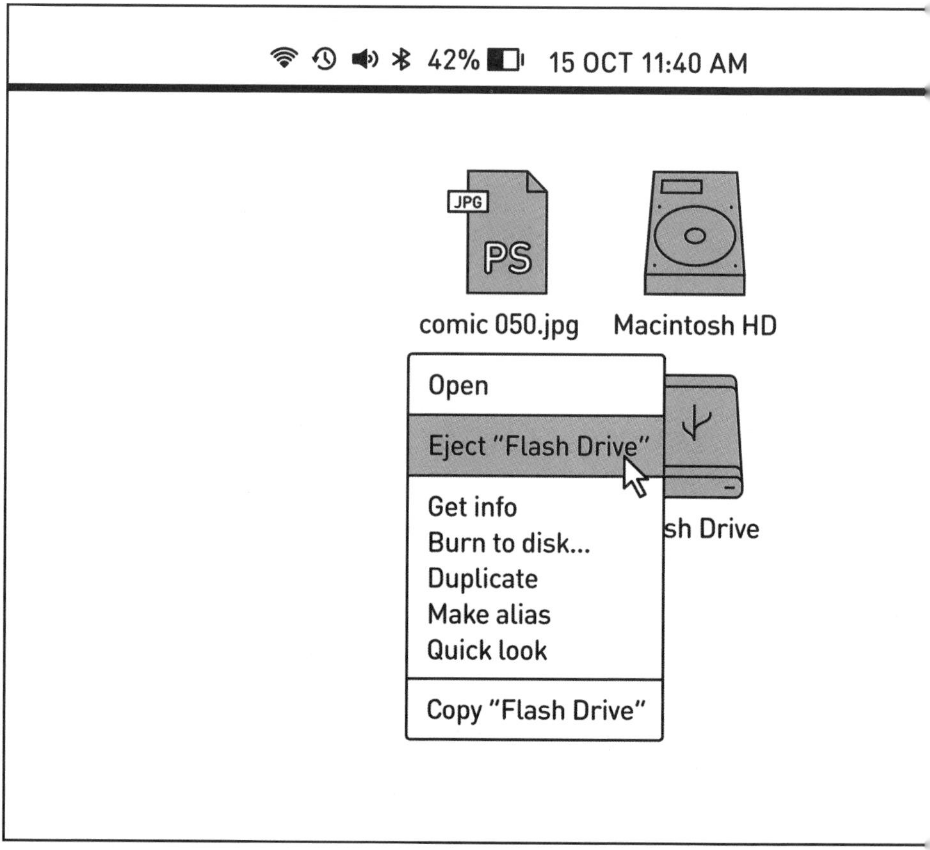

42%
15 OCT 11:40 AM
JPG
PS
comic 050.jpg
Macintosh HD
Open
Eject "Flash Drive"
Get info
Burn to disk...
Duplicate
Make alias
Quick look
Copy "Flash Drive"
sh Drive

comic 050.jpg   Macintosh HD

The disk was not ejected properly.
If possible, always eject a disk
before unplugging it or turning
it off.

OK

🛜 🕘 🔊 ✳ 42% 🔋 15 OCT 11:40 AM

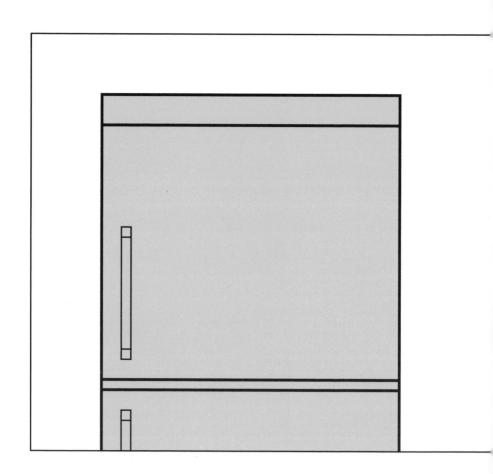

☐ Carry boxes
☐ Hose down patio
☐ Empty garage
☐ Cut grass
☐ Kick back

☒ Carry boxes
☒ Hose down patio
☒ Empty garage
☒ Cut grass
☒ Kick back

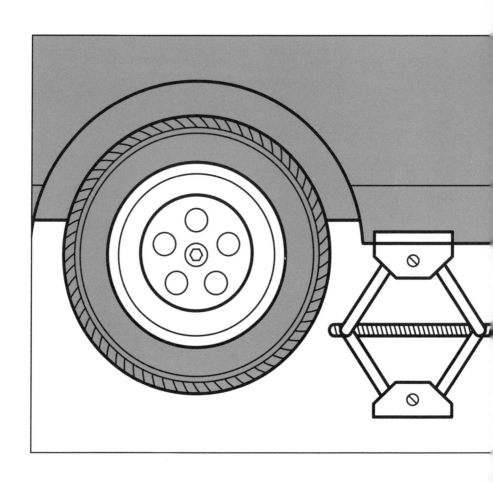

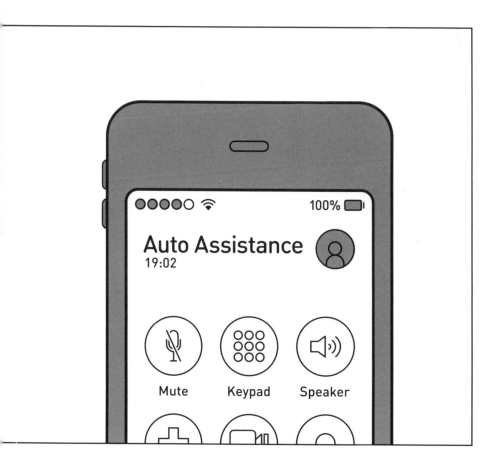

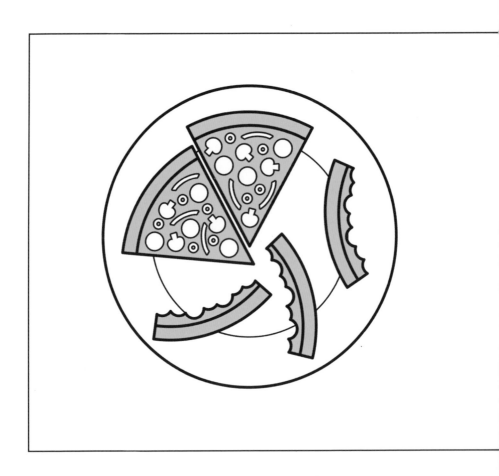

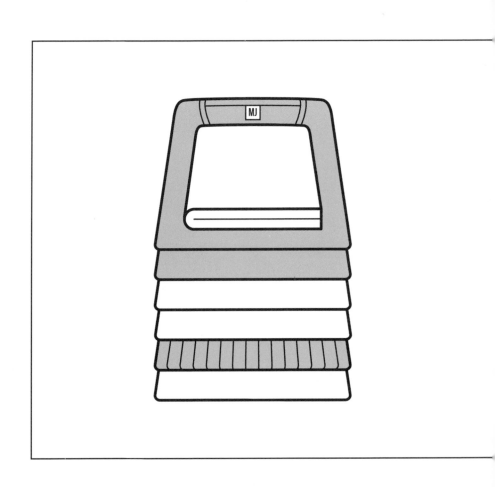

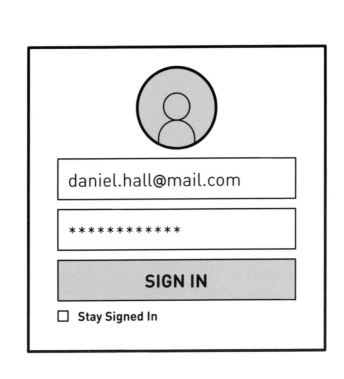

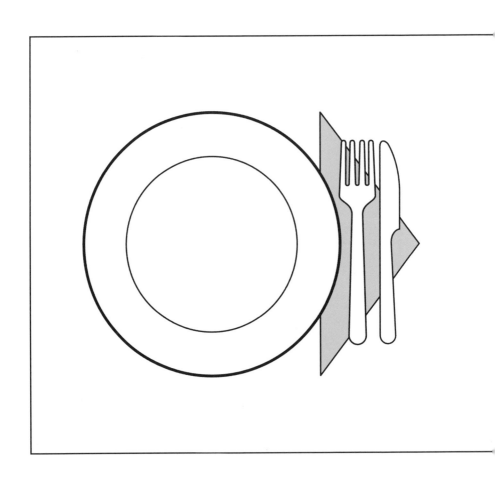

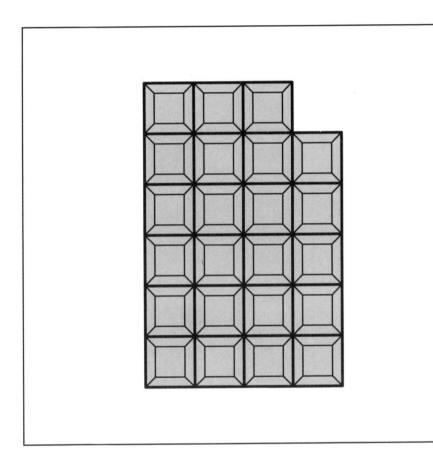

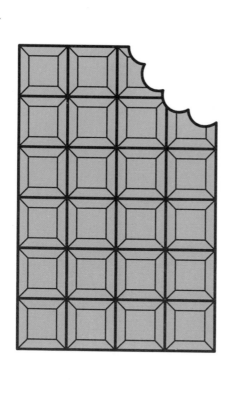

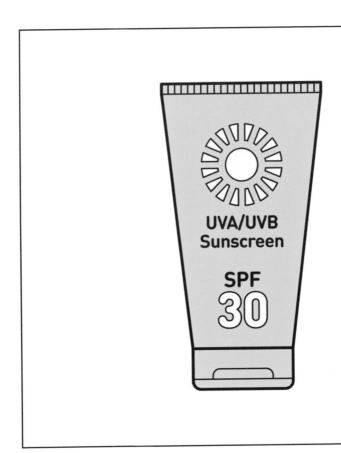

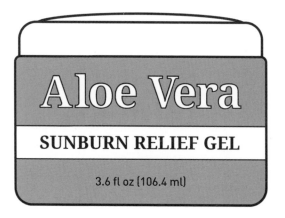

Aloe Vera

SUNBURN RELIEF GEL

3.6 fl oz (106.4 ml)

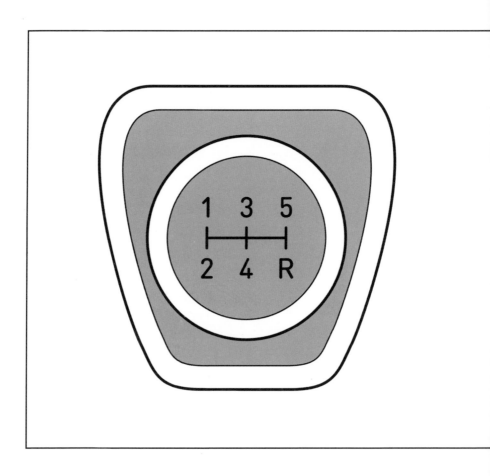

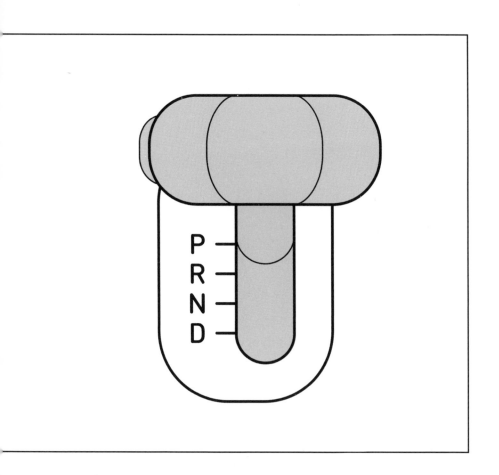

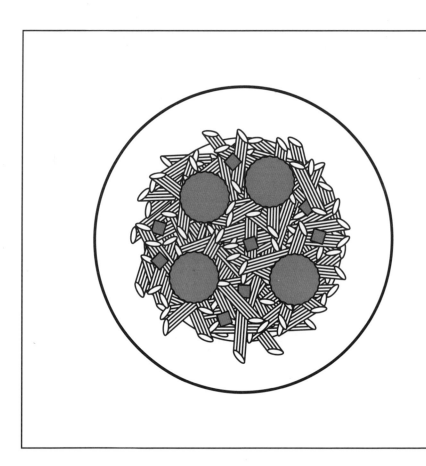

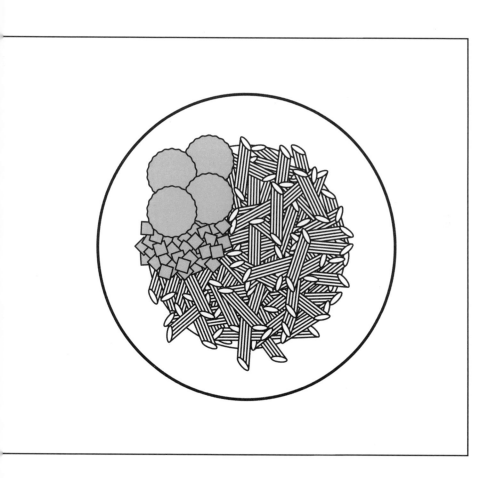

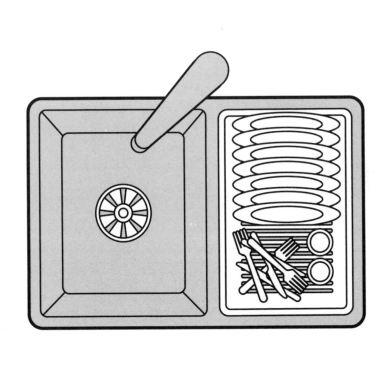

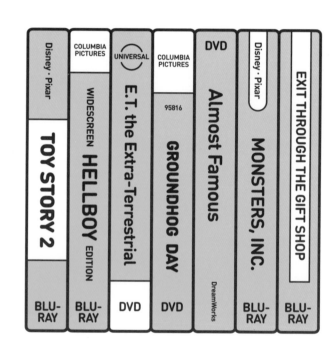

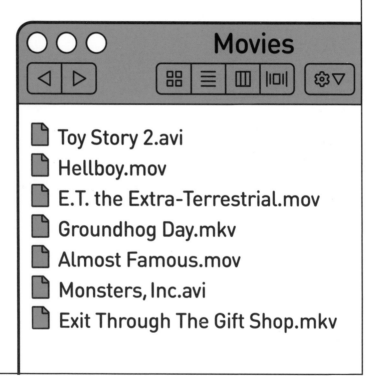

Mon	Tue	Wed	Thu	Fri
				1
4	5	6	7	8
Community Outreach w/ Ron				JK Show
Report w/ Jerry		April's Internship Review		
11	12	13	14	15
Pawnee Zoo Fundraiser			Council Meeting	
Trip to Eagleton				Call Ann
18	19	20	21	22
Pawnee Harvest Festival				
Unity Concert		Clean Restroom Task Force		
25	26	27	28	
State Audit to the Department with Chris				
Fun in the Sun			Sweetums' Meeting	

Mon	Tue	Wed	Thu	Fri
				1
4	5	6	7	8
11	12	13	14	15
18	19	20	21	22
25	26	27	28	

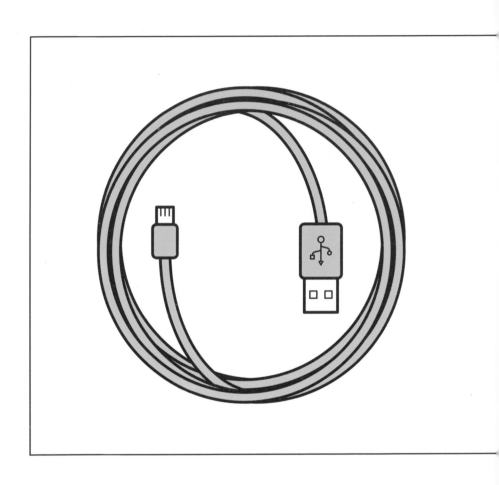

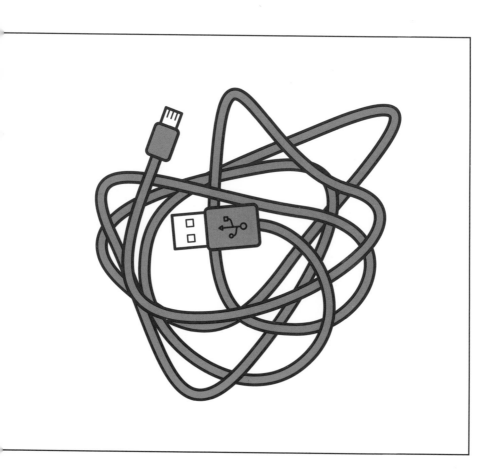

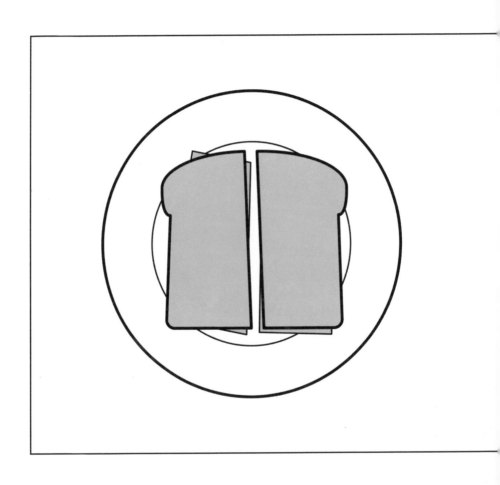

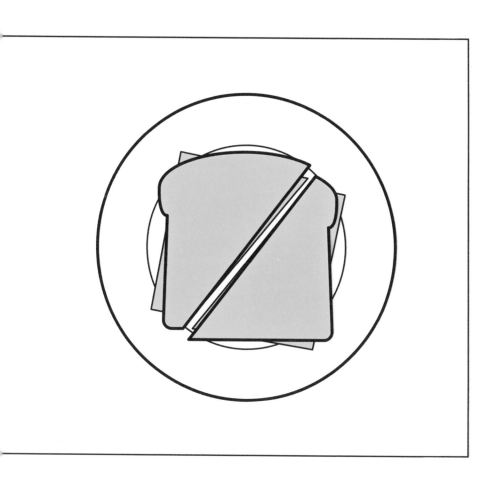

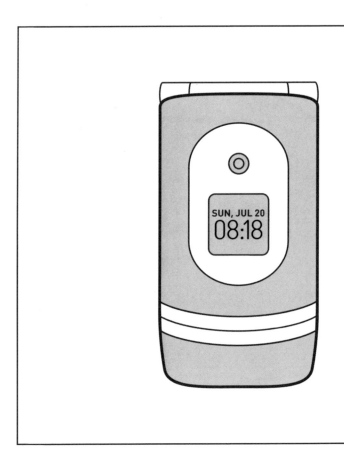

08:18

Sunday, July 20

> Slide to unlock

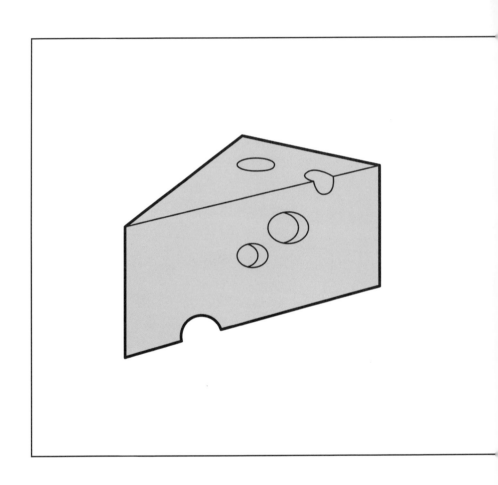

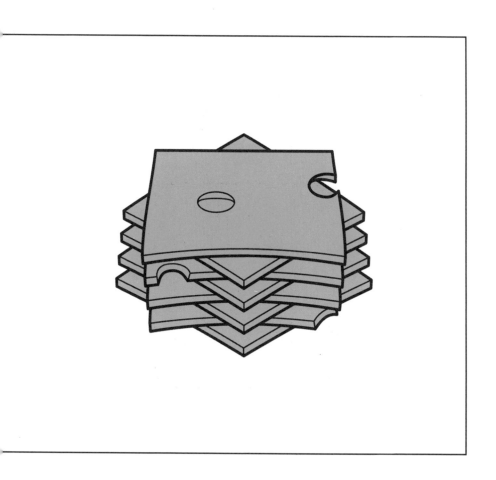

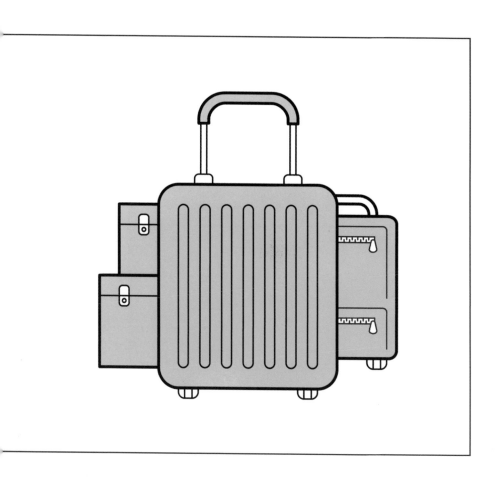

≡	**TODAY**	+
Talk to Marceline		6:00 AM
Invite Jake to lunch		8:45 AM
Meet Finn at Tree Fort Café		12:30 PM
Edit BMO Report		1:00 PM
Rehearse with Billy		2:30 PM

☰	**TODAY**	+
Talk to Marceline		**6:00 PM**
Invite Jake to dinner		**8:45 PM**
Meet Finn at Tree Fort Café		**12:30 AM**
Edit BMO Report		**1:00 AM**
Rehearse with Billy		**2:30 AM**

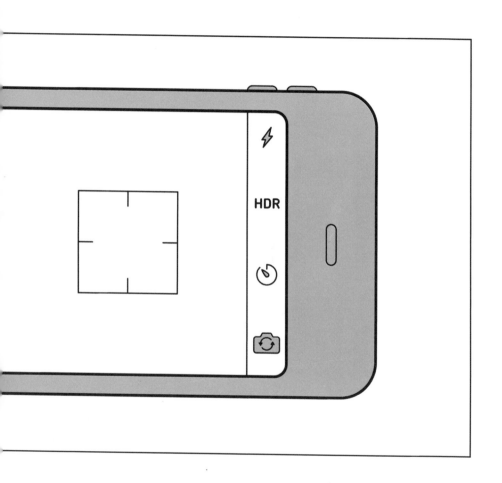

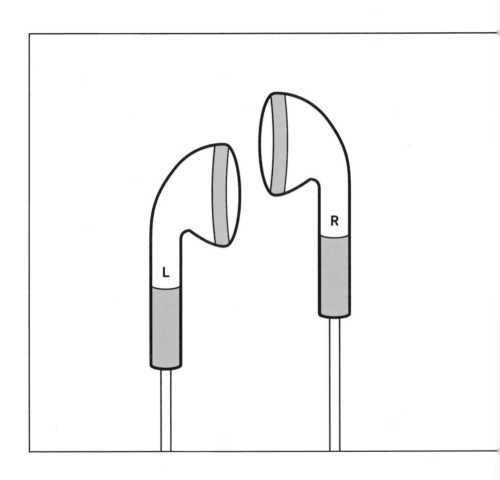

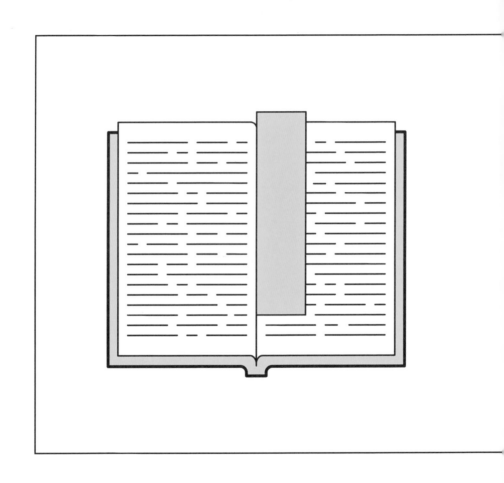

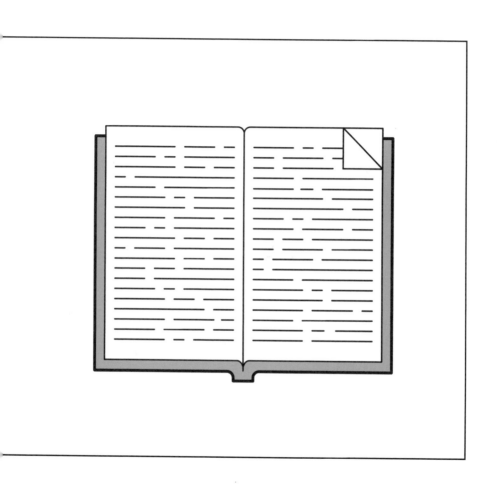

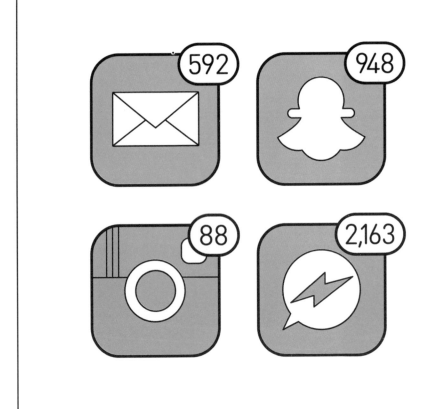

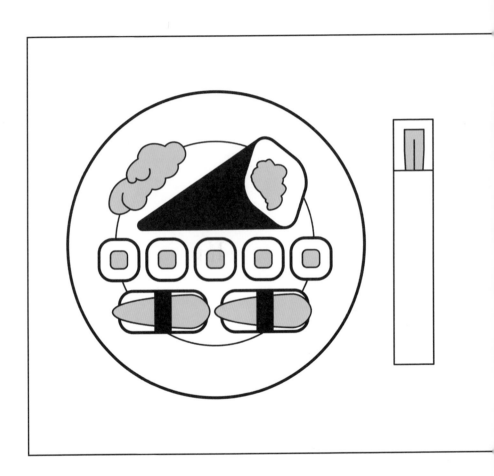

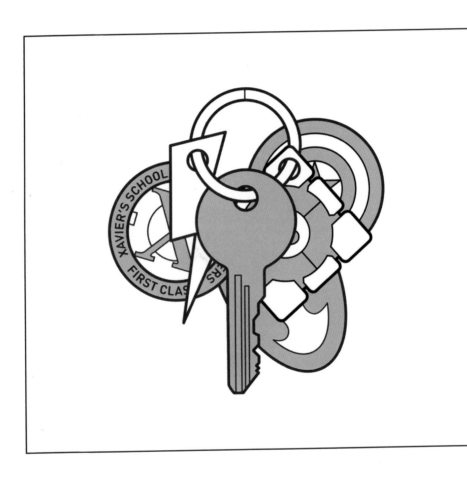

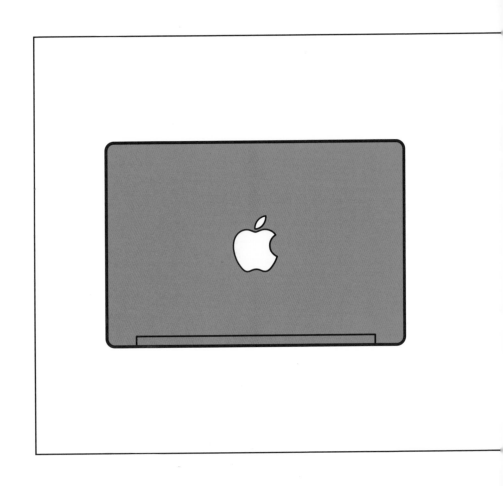

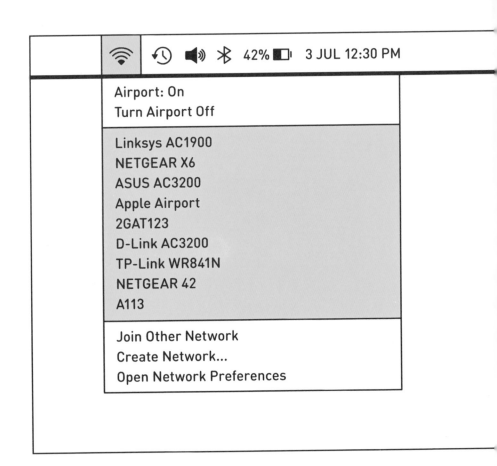

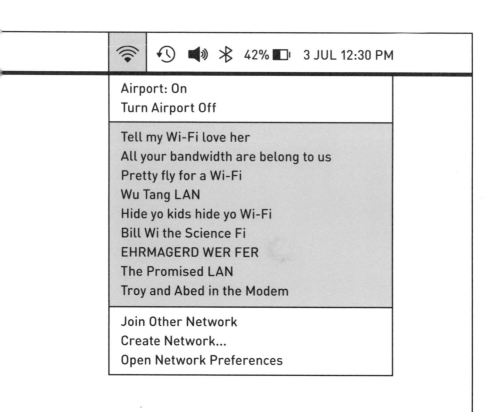

Airport: On
Turn Airport Off

Tell my Wi-Fi love her
All your bandwidth are belong to us
Pretty fly for a Wi-Fi
Wu Tang LAN
Hide yo kids hide yo Wi-Fi
Bill Wi the Science Fi
EHRMAGERD WER FER
The Promised LAN
Troy and Abed in the Modem

Join Other Network
Create Network...
Open Network Preferences

42% 3 JUL 12:30 PM

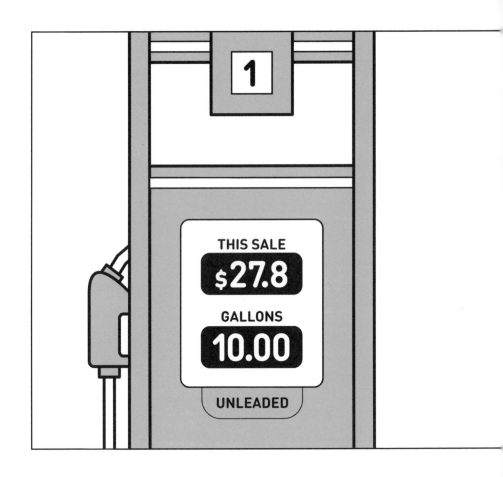

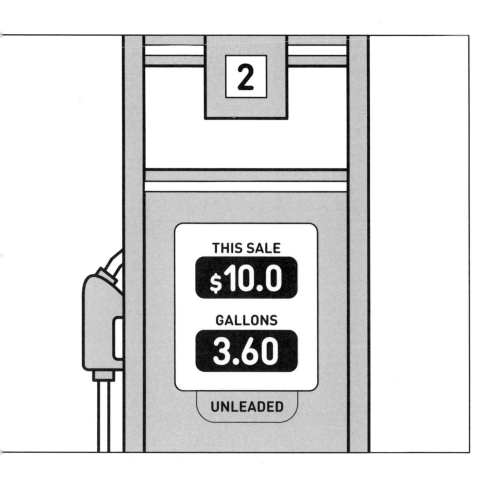

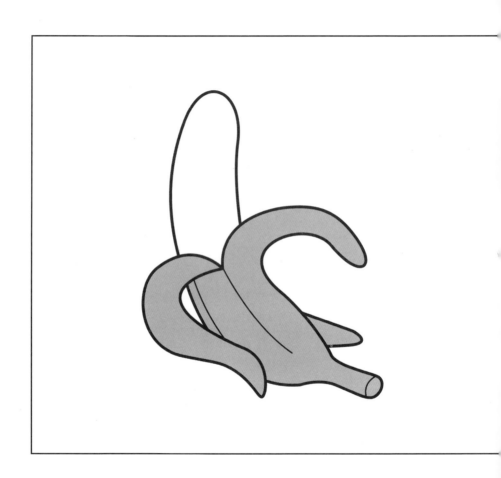

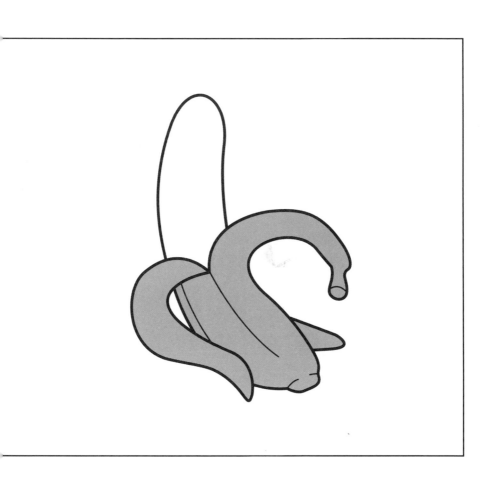

SCALE OF COMPATIBILITY

1–11 MATCHES   Mortal Enemies

Yikes! You agree on pretty much . . . nothing. This bodes well for a lot of lively arguments over inconsequential things, but not so much for a long-lasting relationship. Whatever one of you likes, the other favors the complete opposite. It's not that either of you is right or wrong, it's just that this dynamic tends to be a little infuriating. If you had to choose *one* person to keep you company on a deserted island, you would rather have a volleyball named Wilson than this human. On the other hand, there *is* a very slim chance that you could be a match made in heaven—that one-in-a-million, ride-or-die, other-half kind of bond. So there's that.

12–23 MATCHES   Unsteady Acquaintances

One second, you're on the same wavelength, the next, you're completely blindsided. Because you have so few things in common, emotions could turn at the drop of a hat. But that's what makes life interesting, right? A strong connection here is questionable, though, so it might be best to keep each other at arm's length to avoid potential conflict . . . unless you love to be constantly challenged and surprised. In that case, the two of you will get along just fine.

24–35 MATCHES   Casual Cohorts

You might not hang out that often—in fact, it's probably a rare occurrence. But on those occasions when you do get together, you both feel incredibly refreshed afterward and wonder why you don't do it more often. You are diamonds in the rough to each other. Those magical good times are fun *because* they're so few and far between. You both know better than to force it, which is why this relationship is perfect in its imperfections.